Highlights™
Hidden Pictures®

101
Bananas

Go bananas finding all 101 hidden bananas in this book!

HIGHLIGHTS PRESS
Honesdale, Pennsylvania

W9-DJC-325

Monkey Gymnastics

7 bananas

toothbrush

drinking straw

bat

yo-yo

carrot

hammer

snake

insect

teacup

lollipop

pencil

spoon

paper clip

ladle

ruler

Baking Day

Art by Mary Sullivan

banana

candle

mushroom

dart

boot

purse

pennant

ladder

car

sock

toothbrush

shuttlecock

arrowhead

slice of pie

ring

School of Fish

banana

paper clip

sailboat

glove

ring

book

hat

ice-cream cone

crown

hourglass

toothbrush

shoe

Art by Tim Davis

Flea Market Treasures

banana

slice of bread

bowl

snail

spoon

bird

dog bone

horseshoe

candle

ring

hammer

slice of pizza

pencil

candy cane

needle

envelope

canoe

dog bowl

teacup

fork

pie

magnet

Art by Kelly Kennedy

Otter Olympics

banana

wishbone

spatula

flag

fishhook

mug

eyeglasses

mitten

ruler

ring

slice of pizza

heart

toothbrush

Art by Karen Stormer Brooks

Swamp Monsters

banana

artist's brush

necktie

yo-yo

spoon

slice of pie

pencil

belt

boot

chili pepper

crescent moon

boomerang

mug

stethoscope

Art by Neil Numberman

Sloth Sleepover

banana

musical note

pine tree

comb

artist's brush

pencil

crown

toothbrush

book

feather

slice of pie

turtle

hammer

sailboat

pear

baseball cap

flute

closed umbrella

Art by Jennifer Harney

Peanut Farmer

banana

comb

ring

heart

clothespin

bat

steamboat

ice-cream
cone

fishhook

toothbrush

nail

pencil

Art by Tim Davis

Pizza Party

banana

snail

carrot

party hat

cane

grapes

fan

flashlight

flower

belt

suitcase

clock

ladder

button

butterfly

pine tree

ice-cream cone

pail

seashell

muffin

ladybug

boot

toothbrush

Art by Mernie Gallagher-Cole

Bunnies in Space

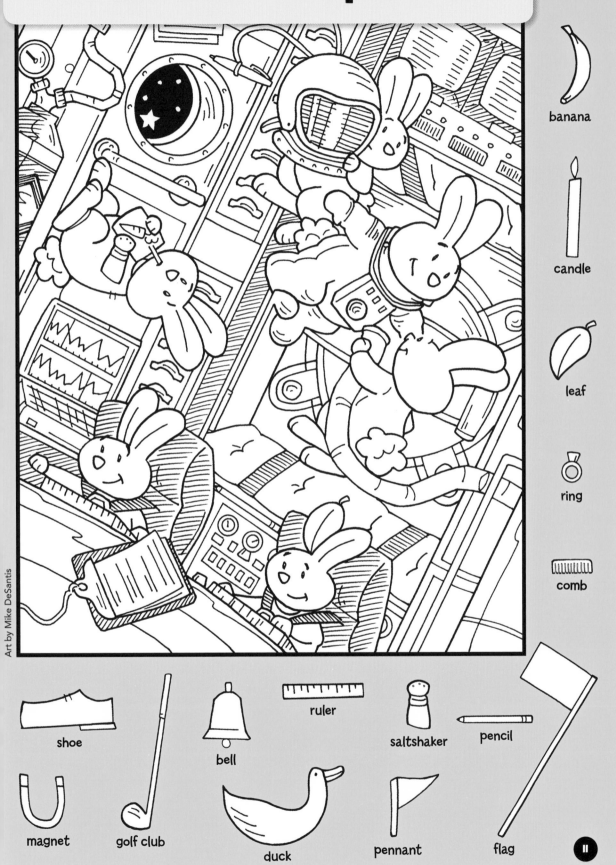

banana

candle

leaf

ring

comb

shoe

bell

ruler

saltshaker

pencil

magnet

golf club

duck

pennant

flag

Look *Whoo*'s Skating

banana

artist's brush

wishbone

trowel

pennant

bell

teacup

boomerang

shoe

leaf

gravy boat

canoe

heart

saucepan

envelope

candle

building block

chili pepper

I'm Open!

banana

football

light bulb

heart

muffin

slice of bread

golf club

adhesive bandage

arrow

wishbone

spool of thread

rolling pin

comb

mushroom

Art by Laura Freeman

Wishy Washy Coin Laundry

banana

ring

crescent
moon

golf club

worm

toothbrush

ruler

kite

slice of pie

book

mug

button

feather

Art by David Helton

So Many Hats

banana

tennis racket

football

bean

fork

paper clip

pail

acorn

key

shoe

balloon

mushroom

car

baseball bat

horseshoe

baby's bottle

kite

scissors

hamburger

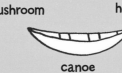
canoe

flashlight

fish

Art by Mernie Gallagher-Cole

Starry Night

Art by Susan T. Hall

banana

slice of pizza

pine tree

heart

bat

angelfish

vase

pen

bird

canoe

needle

artist's brush

basket

wedge of orange

Field Trip

banana

mug

sailboat

duck

sock

needle

snake

toothbrush

beehive

kite

drinking straw

envelope

olive

artist's brush

bowl

flag

coffeepot

baseball bat

pencil

ruler

Art by Deborah Johnson

Bug Band

banana

sock

pennant

ring

bird

teacup

ice-cream
bar

candle

baseball bat

bell

crescent moon

sailboat

Art by Karen Stormer Brooks

Back to School

Art by Rich Powell

banana

sailboat

teacup

bowl

feather

fish

waffle

wedge of cheese

pencil

slice of pie

candle

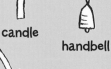
handbell

light bulb

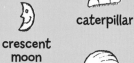
toothbrush

boot

worm

rake

crescent moon

caterpillar

tack

canoe

heart

hatchet

comb

bar of soap

19

Armadillo Party

banana

handbell

heart

paper clip

carrot

egg

coat hanger

megaphone

sailboat

hammer

pencil

fish

chicken

Art by Tim Davis

Snow Birds

banana

tack

carrot

artist's brush

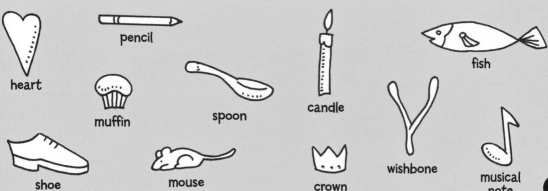

heart

pencil

muffin

spoon

candle

fish

shoe

mouse

crown

wishbone

musical note

Rock Climbers

banana

candle

sock

golf club

crescent moon

fishhook

slice of bread

shoe

frying pan

oar

fish

spoon

needle

bell

pennant

Art by Mike DeSantis

Bird Bath

Art by Deborah Johnson

banana

ice-cream cone

peanut

party hat

crayon

handbell

sheep

piece of candy

light bulb

teacup

baseball bat

heart

mushroom

coffeepot

envelope

artist's brush

star

mitten

button

hat

23

Penguin Pool

banana

clothespin

mitten

shovel

iron

bottle

closed
umbrella

flag

hamburger

toothbrush

cherry

canoe

lemon

mushroom

hoe

tube of
toothpaste

saltshaker

record

key

pine tree

Art by Laura Ferraro Close

Off the Leash

 banana

 screwdriver

 pencil

 heart

 bell

 slice of bread

candy corn

 glove

 open book

toothbrush

 spoon

 feather

 comb

 earmuffs

artist's brush

Art by Janet McDonnell

Hippo Checkup

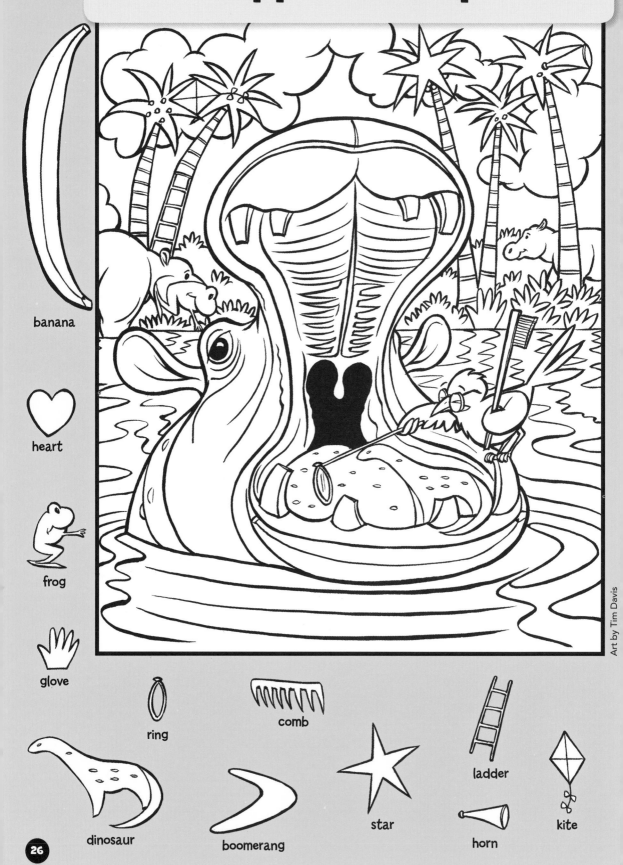

banana

heart

frog

glove

ring

comb

dinosaur

boomerang

star

ladder

horn

kite

Art by Tim Davis

26

Science Fair

banana

carrot

teacup

artist's brush

cookie

olive

magic wand

leaf

hockey stick

crescent moon

crown

boomerang

magnet

fish

canoe

flag

envelope

doughnut

ghost

ruler

bell

sock

snake

needle

Art by Bill Golliher

SCIENCE FAIR

JUDGE

Neck to Neck

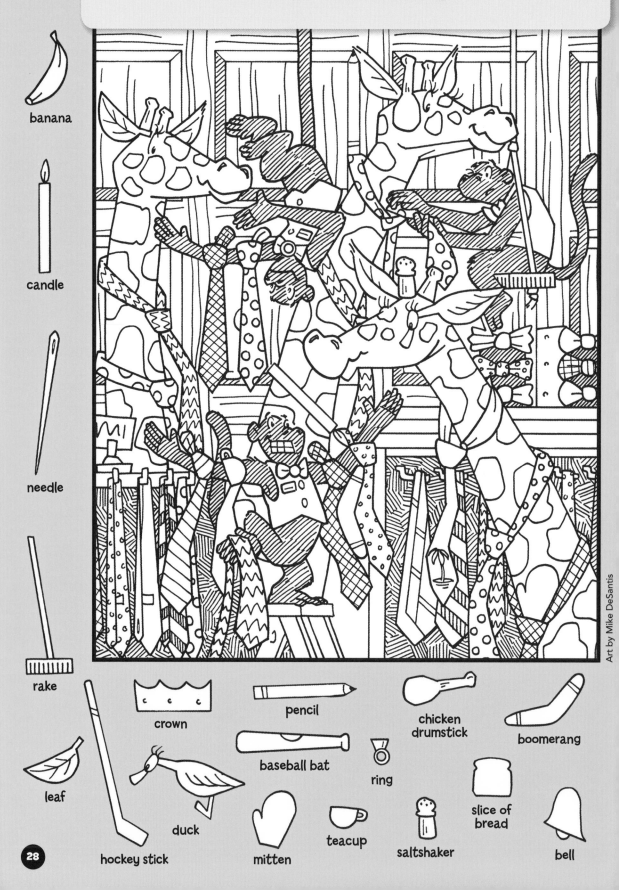

banana

candle

needle

rake

crown

pencil

chicken drumstick

boomerang

leaf

baseball bat

ring

slice of bread

hockey stick

duck

mitten

teacup

saltshaker

bell

Art by Mike DeSantis

Planetarium Day

Art by Diana Zourelias

banana
heart
flag
wishbone
yo-yo
bowl

potato
hockey stick
bean
golf tee
saucepan
magnet
elf's hat
pencil
crayon
lollipop
doughnut
funnel
bell
butterfly
teacup
sailboat
book
rolling pin
spool of thread
stick of gum
snowman
slice of pizza
flowerpot

Toucan Treat

banana

kite

pen

scissors

dog

bell

caterpillar

whale

needle

fish

pencil

mouse

Art by Susan T. Hall

Whee!

banana

ring

fork

nail

artist's brush

needle

butterfly

kite

horseshoe

sailboat

ice-cream cone

slice of pie

toothbrush

sock

pencil

muffin

Art by Karen Stormer Brooks

Doggy Dilemma

banana

flag

worm

baseball
bat

Art by Ethan Long

open book

slice of pizza

mouse

domino

envelope

slice of
watermelon

dog bone

heart

Frog Fun

banana

star

wishbone

fork

lollipop

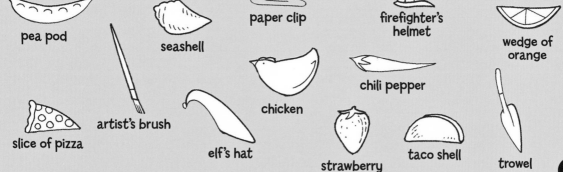

pea pod

seashell

paper clip

firefighter's helmet

wedge of orange

chili pepper

chicken

slice of pizza

artist's brush

elf's hat

strawberry

taco shell

trowel

Art by Gary Mohrman

The Neighs Have It

banana

hockey stick

domino

ladder

candy cane

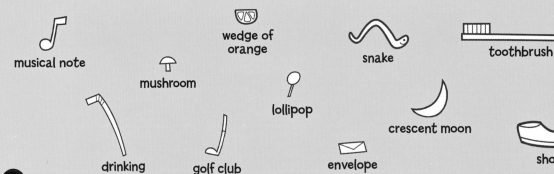

musical note

mushroom

wedge of orange

lollipop

snake

toothbrush

drinking straw

golf club

envelope

crescent moon

shoe

Art by Gary LaCoste

Skateboarders

banana

carrot

calculator

toothbrush

barbell

crown

star

fish

heart

rabbit

bowl

pencil

crescent moon

slice of pizza

Art by Apryl Stott

35

Carousel Ride

banana

candy cane

heart

traffic light

lollipop

handbell

crown

mug

wristwatch

pine tree

hairbrush

bowl

tulip

artist's brush

dragonfly

muffin

snail

musical note

whale

pencil

mushroom

Art by Jennifer Harney

Wild Tales

Art by Kelly Kennedy

banana

hat

button

comb

lollipop

scissors

kite

flyswatter

fried egg

glove

crayon

fish

paper clip

arrow

eyeglasses

snail

toothbrush

broccoli

The Robot

banana

grapes

apple

pear

carrot

pineapple

cherry

peanut

ear of corn

bean

mushroom

slice of
watermelon

Art by Joseph Wigfield

Log Rolling

Art by Gary Mohrman

banana

wishbone

mushroom

crescent moon

lightning bolt

candle

sponge

feather

glove

funnel

muffin

cane

pennant

butter knife

hamburger

needle

snake

heart

tulip

peanut

39

Tug of War

Art by Rocky Fuller

banana

ladder

candy
cane

shovel

drinking
straw

heart

tea bag

envelope

fishhook

wrench

ladle

pencil

funnel

magnet

hamburger

screw

mug

Art Museum

banana

crescent moon

cherry

candle

pencil

baseball

sock

lollipop

wedge of orange

slice of pizza

crown

button

clock

party hat

fishhook

seashell

whale

spoon

envelope

Art by Mernie Gallagher-Cole

Swimming Trunks

banana

ladder

needle

open book

rabbit

celery

ladle

snake

sock

horseshoe

apple

funnel

wedge of orange

Art by Karen Stormer Brooks

Dino Sock Hop

Art by Deborah Johnson

banana

ring

peanut

pennant

artist's brush

feather

boot

sailboat

scissors

horseshoe

fish

light bulb

baseball

glove

barbell

party hat

carrot

hatchet

bowl

Kite Flight

banana

chef's hat

glove

bow tie

drinking straw

Art by Scot Ritchie

comb

horseshoe

spatula

slice of pizza

canoe

sheep

table-tennis paddle

paper clip

ring

snake

44

In-Line Ostrich

banana

ice-cream cone

bell

crescent moon

slice of cake

teacup

sailboat

spoon

heart

crown

eyeglasses

glove

fish

toothbrush

Art by Tim Davis

45

Cat Camp

banana

bowling pin

scissors

ice-cream cone

ice-cream bar

heart

carrot

watering can

muffin

traffic cone

needle

toothbrush

mitten

ladle

teacup

magnet

artist's brush

slice of pizza

kite

book

sailboat

Art by Jennifer Harney

Cheering Crocs

Art by Mike DeSantis

banana

fork

golf club

cup and straw

fishhook

flag

flashlight

wishbone

open book

spoon

saltshaker

fish

teacup

ruler

toothbrush

pencil

crescent moon

parrot

tube of toothpaste

needle

crown

comb

Hamster Playhouse

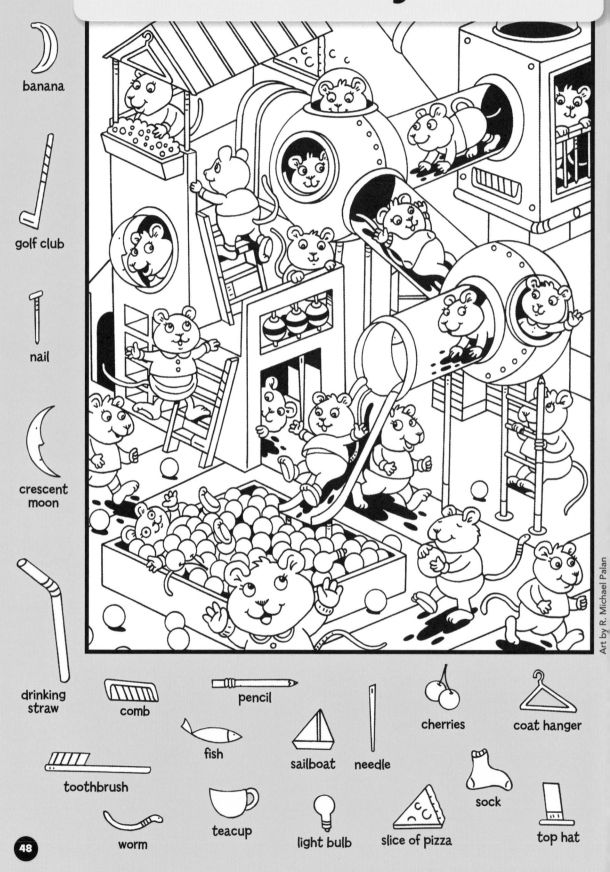

banana

golf club

nail

crescent moon

drinking straw

comb

pencil

cherries

coat hanger

fish

sailboat

needle

toothbrush

teacup

light bulb

slice of pizza

sock

worm

top hat

Art by R. Michael Palan

48

Songbirds

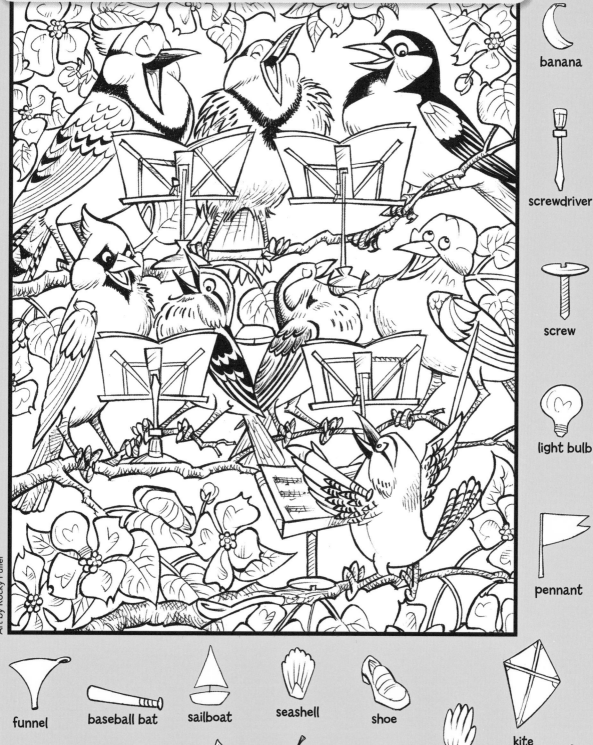

banana

screwdriver

screw

light bulb

pennant

funnel

baseball bat

sailboat

seashell

shoe

glove

kite

pencil

slice of pie

candle

apple core

pitcher

spoon

Art by Rocky Fuller

Rapid Rafters

banana

slice of pie

pencil

spoon

teacup

carrot

handbell

heart

slice of pizza

turtle

toothbrush

glove

Art by Tim Davis

Puzzling Fun

Art by Ron Leiser

banana

nutcracker

coin

bell

rope

wishbone

funnel

toothbrush

pencil

caterpillar

drinking straw

glove

hairbrush

bowl

heart

51

Greener Grass

banana

musical note

artist's brush

ice-cream cone

mitten

fish

toothbrush

saw

mushroom

teacup

paper clip

heart

Art by Tim Davis

52

Pond Explorers

Art by Laura Ferraro Close

banana

lightning bolt

crescent moon

heart

ice-cream cone

ring

apple

flowerpot

mug

light bulb

crayon

raindrop

hairbrush

horn

sock

butterfly

crown

bell

snake

Horseshoe Shopping

banana

balloon

sailboat

bowling pin

leaf

envelope

mushroom

party hat

crown

ruler

flower

slice of pizza

Art by Tamara Petrosino

54

Strike!

HONESDALE ZOO BASEBALL STARS

Art by David Helton

banana

spider

worm

ring

golf club

toothbrush

spoon

button

ruler

envelope

crescent moon

house

bell

mug

sailboat

Space Store

banana

spoon

golf club

kite

button

Super Charged BATTERIES 2112

Art by David Helton

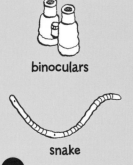
binoculars

stamp

ring

book

ladle

envelope

sock

snake

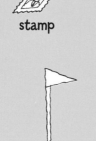
pennant

teacup

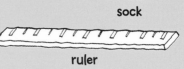
ruler

Ocean Treasure

banana

carrot

paper clip

spoon

egg

paintbrush

bird

hammer

shoe

mushroom

toothbrush

magnet

eyeglasses

Art by Tim Davis

57

Construction Crew

banana

golf club

drinking straw

needle

shovel

funnel

ring

carrot

nail

teacup

heart

candle

open book

tack

toothbrush

pencil

snake

baseball bat

Art by R. Michael Palan

Bunny Hop

banana

crescent moon

bell

nail

vase

heart

whale

teacup

cookie

seashell

acorn

sweet potato

feather

pencil

musical note

tomato

envelope

snake

Art by Gary Mohrman

Hawaiian Hibernation

banana

heart

sock

feather

eyeglasses

horn

scissors

stepladder

ring

kite

ice-cream cone

lizard

teacup

open book

sailboat

Art by Tim Davis

Game Night

banana

sailboat

candle

button

crescent moon

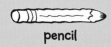
pencil

toothbrush

flying disk

pennant

slice of pie

paintbrush

feather

envelope

spatula

Art by David Helton

Face Painting

banana

sock

horseshoe

candle

ladder

hockey stick

drinking glass

crescent moon

mitten

boot

pencil

slice of pizza

toothbrush

mug

hat

ring

ruler

spoon

caterpillar

carrot

Art by Karen Stormer Brooks

Swimming Ducks

banana

snake

spider

crown

candle

Art by David Helton

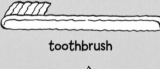
toothbrush

pencil

plate

envelope

kite

button

spoon

Chicken Crossing

banana

heart

tack

paper clip

bell

needle

slice of pie

fish

sailboat

megaphone

toothbrush

pencil

glove

eyeglasses

Art by Tim Davis

Bug Burgers

Art by Laura Ferraro Close

banana

horseshoe

jellyfish

artist's brush

glove

football

fried egg

slice of pizza

needle

teacup

yo-yo

pea pod

bow tie

skateboard

slice of bread

tube of toothpaste

Dino Museum

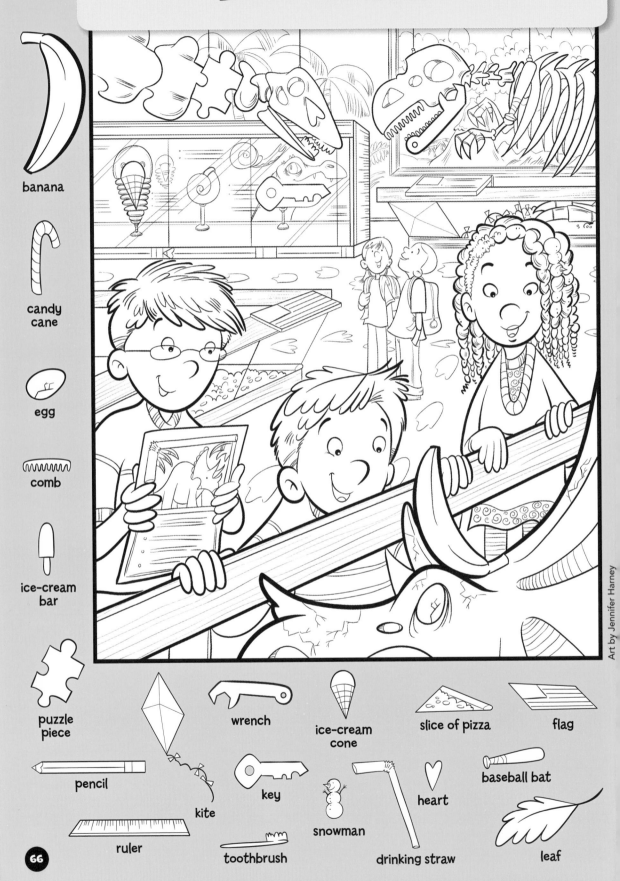

banana

candy cane

egg

comb

ice-cream bar

puzzle piece

pencil

kite

ruler

wrench

key

toothbrush

ice-cream cone

snowman

slice of pizza

drinking straw

heart

flag

baseball bat

leaf

Art by Jennifer Harney

Which Way Is Home?

banana

olive

peanut

carrot

lollipop

chili pepper

doughnut

pretzel

slice of bread

grapes

acorn

teacup

apple core

wishbone

Art by Rocky Fuller

Piggy Pirouette

banana

nail

teacup

snail

needle

button

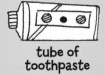
tube of
toothpaste

boot

butterfly

sailboat

heart

bowl

fish

pear

Bat Cave

banana

teacup

mitten

bell

sailboat

cowboy hat

paper clip

bird

tooth

glove

horn

fish

boomerang

ice-cream cone

Feeding the Fish

banana

beehive

wedge of orange

crescent moon

acorn

candle

comb

harmonica

flashlight

sailboat

wedge of cheese

drumstick

envelope

hockey stick

elf's hat

crown

ruler

Art by Patrick Girouard

70

Jungle Boogie

banana

fishhook

dog dish

candle

bell

elf's hat

pennant

crescent moon

starfish

belt

domino

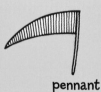
dolphin

pine tree

ring

sailboat

Art by Gary Mohrman

71

Up and Away!

banana

glove

crescent moon

candy cane

magnet

Art by Rocky Fuller

computer

musical note

can opener

pencil

sailboat

needle

spool of thread

spoon

football

Dog Show

banana

ice-cream bar

nail

wishbone

heart

book

party hat

bowl

pinecone

mallet

shoe

pencil

Art by Mary Sullivan

Manatee Bay

banana

fork

sock

heart

ice pop

button

mouse

teacup

umbrella

fried egg

bird

spoon

tulip

baseball bat

Art by Maggie Swanson

Bunny Bedtime

banana

candle

pennant

golf club

crescent moon

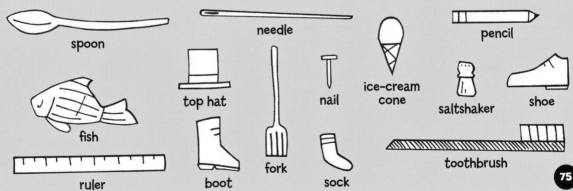

spoon

needle

pencil

fish

top hat

nail

ice-cream cone

saltshaker

shoe

ruler

boot

fork

sock

toothbrush

Art by Mike DeSantis

Tents Up

banana

pennant

hockey stick

bowl

artist's brush

lollipop

crayon

toothbrush

shoe

ice-cream cone

glove

lamp

candle

spoon

Art by Mary Sullivan

Space Traffic

banana

potato

hot dog

ghost

horseshoe

pine tree

bowl

sailboat

flower

feather

wedge of orange

lemon

cherry

wristwatch

slice of pizza

doughnut

broom

four-leaf clover

yo-yo

book

fried egg

Dino Dunk

banana

ice-cream cone

balloon

scissors

bell

rollerskate

snake

sailboat

crown

bird

carrot

teacup

eyeglasses

Art by Tim Davis

Paddock Pals

Art by Christine Schneider

banana

fish

fried egg

nail

funnel

pencil

ring

ruler

feather

lollipop

sailboat

snake

Pig Pyramid

banana

heart

golf club

teacup

button

candle

crayon

spoon

bat

teapot

mitten

pencil

wishbone

shoe

crown

artist's brush

crescent moon

sock

Art by Mike DeSantis

Family Dinner

banana

golf club

clothespin

snail

candle

drinking straw

needle

tack

envelope

glove

mug

crescent moon

pencil

slice of pie

binoculars

Art by Chuck Dillon

Monster Matinee

banana

lemon

tack

golf club

pennant

spatula

 spoon

envelope

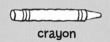 crayon

 domino

 bell

 ruler

 bowl

 button

 sock

Art by David Helton

Under Umbrellas

banana

spoon

mug

candle

paper clip

bat

book

ring

shovel

tack

bell

slice of pizza

megaphone

sailboat

needle

snake

heart

crown

Art by Tim Davis

Ant Farm

banana

lollipop

fishhook

needle

nail

pencil

spoon

coat hanger

toothbrush

candle

carrot

spatula

teacup

Art by R. Michael Palan

Dog Wash

banana

horseshoe

top hat

envelope

crayon

lemon

snake

boomerang

button

muffin

spoon

belt

bell

adhesive
bandage

slipper

fried egg

Art by Mernie Gallagher-Cole

85

Arctic Shoppers

banana

pennant

yo-yo

crescent moon

hockey stick

sock

trumpet

heart

bell

hairbrush

hat

ruler

slice of pie

pointy hat

crayon

key

window

comb

crown

candle

shovel

Art by Laura Ferraro Close

Dino Dinner

banana

feather

eyeglasses

sailboat

ice-cream cone

bowl

cinnamon bun

toothbrush

button

slice of pie

cat

slice of pizza

snake

pencil

scissors

Art by Susan T. Hall

Riding Trail

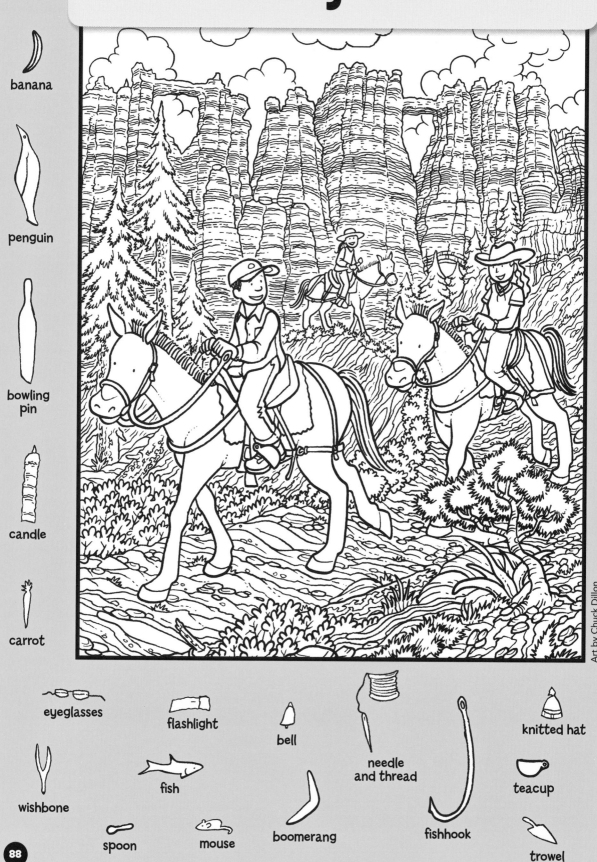

banana

penguin

bowling pin

candle

carrot

eyeglasses

flashlight

bell

needle and thread

knitted hat

wishbone

fish

teacup

spoon

mouse

boomerang

fishhook

trowel

Art by Chuck Dillon

Car Wash

banana

fishhook

ring

paper clip

hourglass

crescent moon

cane

mallet

sailboat

comb

pennant

can

bow

baton

button

boot

tulip

golf club

sneaker

crown

footprint

butter knife

needle

A Day at the Zoo

banana

magnet

book

fork

glove

eyeglasses

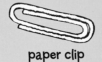

paper clip

crayon

arrow

rolling pin

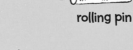

crown

magnifying glass

Job Site at Night

 banana

drinking straw

carrot

sailboat

ladder

 lollipop

 hockey stick

 heart

pencil

piece of popcorn

envelope

comb

wedge of orange

 candy cane

waffle

 crown

 golf club

artist's brush

fishhook

 slice of pizza

 pennant

toothbrush

 megaphone

magnifying glass

 bowl

 horseshoe

Picking Pumpkins

banana

drinking straw

sock

mushroom

crescent moon

button

pail

candle

fish

pencil

mitten

comb

ruler

bell

shoe

spatula

artist's brush

musical note

wishbone

baseball cap

nail

Art by Mike DeSantis

Space Surfing

banana

needle

ladle

trowel

cactus

wishbone

tube of
toothpaste

worm

sock

ghost

fish

flashlight

ring

Art by R. Michael Palan

93

Nature Center

banana

necktie

golf club

ring

ice-cream bar

fork

pencil

pail

football

crayon

candy corn

arrow

sock

flowerpot

bell

sailboat

green bean

Art by Laura Ferraro Close

Sailing

Art by Karen Stormer Brooks

banana

needle

party hat

hockey stick

duck

muffin

carrot

flashlight

frying pan

ring

hoe

teacup

spoon

Monkey Jungle Gym

banana
snail
pennant
comb
artist's brush
needle
tack
closed umbrella
heart
crescent moon
fishhook
pineapple
lightning bolt
magnet
key
fan
caterpillar
ladder
screw
shuttlecock
pencil
seashell
butterfly
drum
slice of pie
musical note
light bulb
book
handbag
acorn
slice of bread
saltshaker
crown
scissors
snake
arrow
sailboat
ring
pear
piece of popcorn

SLIDE

Art by Diana Zourelias

Go Bananas!

Did you find all 101 bananas? A Hidden Pictures® super sleuth like you deserves a treat! That's why we've added a bunch of bonus activities on the following pages, ripe for the picking.

But before you take a bite out of these puzzles, see if you can unpeel the answers to these questions, looking back at the puzzles you just solved.

Which fruit can you find the most of?

There are 27 spoons just waiting for a banana split. Can you find them all?

Would you rather have a slice of bread or a muffin? Banana flavored, of course! Which tasty treat are there more of?

Laugh Out Loud

How do monkeys go downstairs?
They slide down the bananaster.

Brad: Why would a bear paint its face yellow?
Chad: I don't know. Why?
Brad: So it can hide in a banana tree.
Chad: Impossible! I've never seen a bear in a banana tree.
Brad: See? It works!

What do you call a mean banana with brown spots?
Rotten

What do you call a banana with wings?
A fruit fly

Man: Why do you have a banana in your ear?
Clown: I'm sorry. I can't hear you. I have a banana in my ear.

What is the best time to eat a banana?
When the moment is ripe

"Bananas? You prescribe bananas for everything!"

Why did the monkey eat so many bananas?
He liked them a bunch.

Snack Time

Here are two tasty recipes to try!

Banana People

apple → blueberry →

strawberry → raisin →

celery →

Use cream cheese or peanut butter as "glue."

pretzel → carrot →

By Jill B. Dillon • Art by Kevin Zimmer

Banana-Strawberry Milkshakes

1. Ask an adult to help slice 1 **banana** and 4 large **strawberries**. Put the banana and strawberries in a blender.

2. Add 2 scoops of **vanilla ice cream** and 2 cups of **milk**. Have an adult help blend the ingredients until the mixture is smooth.

3. Pour into a glass, and top with **whipped cream**. Enjoy your milkshake!

A milkshake mustache is a must-have!

Art by Mike Moran

Banana Phones

Follow each monkey's phone vine to see who's talking to whom.

What did the banana say to the monkey?
Nothing. Bananas can't talk!

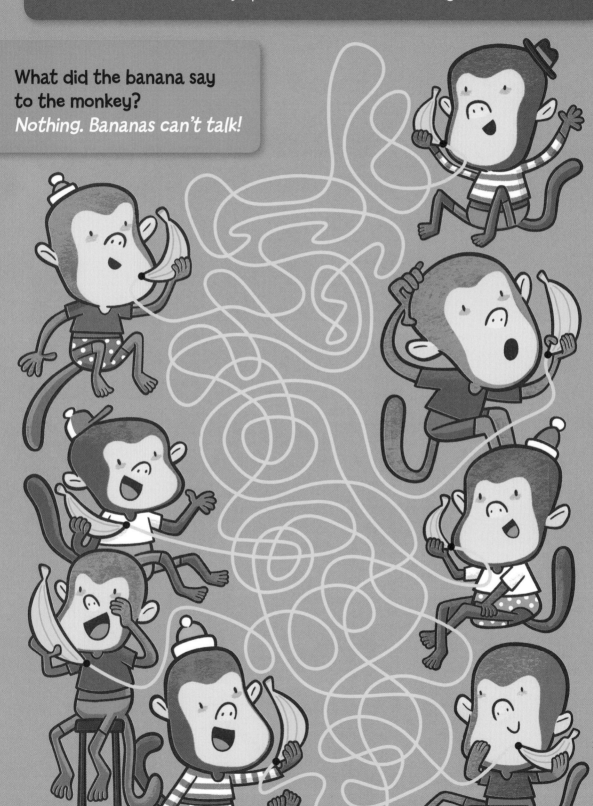

Art by Erica Sirotich

Fruit Find

There are **20** fruit words hidden in this grid—up, down, across, backward, and diagonally. We found BANANA. Can you find the rest?

```
P L U M Y V X E B Z C C E R C
K E K I B A N A N A T X L K G
B Y R R E B W A R T S L J R I
A N A T M T J S P S M H W Z F
H P Y L I M E D E W A U C M P
M F P U M R U P A N N C U X E
Z J D L N O A M C A G K E M A
N Z F O E R R S H N O L E M R
F B M L G C Z A P U M E A C D
N E X J B X I T N B J B M H C
L N T O C I R P A G E E A E H
G R A P E F R U I T E R S R G
U U I O P A P A Y A I R R R T
I E N M D N M B C X H Y O Y R
G W M K I W I S R T S K W K E
```

Word List

APPLE	GRAPEFRUIT	LIME	PEACH
APRICOT	GRAPES	MANGO	PEAR
~~BANANA~~	HUCKLEBERRY	MELON	PLUM
CHERRY	KIWI	ORANGE	RASPBERRY
FIG	LEMON	PAPAYA	STRAWBERRY

Lunch at The Banana Café

Max is meeting his friends for lunch at The Banana Café. If he chooses one appetizer, one main dish, and one dessert, what can he order that will cost exactly $10? How many combinations can you find?

Appetizers

Banana Smoothie	$2.50
Banana Bread	$2.00
Banana Fritter	$3.00
Banana Crêpe	$3.75

Main Dishes

Grilled Banana Sandwich	$4.25
Banana Tacos	$3.00
BBQ Bananas	$5.50
Banana Fruit Salad	$4.00

Desserts

Frozen Bananas	$2.00
Banana Split	$3.25
Banana Cream Pie	$4.00
Banana Custard Cupcake	$2.75

Each of Max's friends is planning to order a different dessert. Use the clues below to figure out who will eat what.

- Monte would like the most expensive dessert.

- Millie had a banana smoothie for an appetizer, so she doesn't want to order anything frozen for dessert.

- Miko's dessert costs $1.25 more than Mei's dessert.

Banana Search

Things are bananas at this grocery store! Can you find **10** bananas in this scene?

Banana Facts

Bananas float in water.

The strings on a banana are called *phloem* (pronounced FLOM).

Bananas do not grow on trees. The banana plant is actually a giant herb.

A cluster of bananas is called a "hand."
Each cluster contains between 10 and 20 bananas, called "fingers."

The bananas we eat were created by humans.
Wild bananas contain large, hard seeds.

An inexpensive way to polish patent leather
shoes is to use the inside of a banana peel!

India is the world's leading producer of bananas.
The top four after that are China, the Philippines, Ecuador, and Brazil.

Bananas are a rich source of vitamin B6, which is good for your brain!

Monkey Business

Three rare monkeys are on display at the local zoo. The middle-aged monkey is three times as old as the youngest monkey. The oldest monkey is twice as old as the middle-aged monkey. The sum of their ages equals 70. Can you help Zookeeper Zack figure out how old the monkeys are? He knows that the youngest monkey is 7 years old.

Art by Tim Beaumont

Fruit Code

There are three jokes about fruit on this page.
Use the picture code to fill in the letters and finish the jokes.

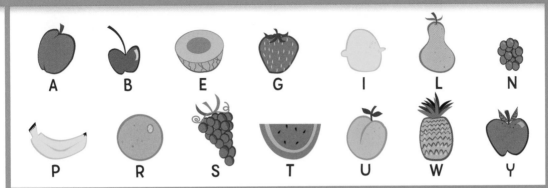

Why did the orange go to the doctor?

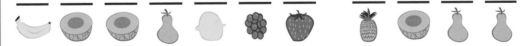

What are bananas best at in gymnastics?

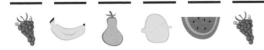

What are twins' favorite fruit?

Brain Starters

START HERE
Take your brain on a hike.
How far can you go?

What would you write in a poem about a banana?

Name three places where you might see both **oranges** and **bananas**.

Where would you be **surprised** to see a banana?

Name

foods that are yellow.

Could **scissors** be used to slice **A BANANA?** How?

What letters of the alphabet could you make with bananas?

How are a **coat** and a **banana peel** alike?

How are they different?

Which fruits would be easiest to **juggle?**

Which would be hardest?

If a banana had a **superpower,** what would it be?

Name a few fruits in order of their juiciness.

THE END

Do you think animals eat **dessert?**

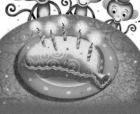

Fruit Salad

Find the hidden fruit in each sentence.

Example: My sweet tooth makes **me lon**g for candy.

1. "One more lap, please," said the coach.

2. A trip to Waikiki will be fun.

3. Kate and Penelope are best friends.

4. Eli meant to water the plants, but he forgot.

5. Please stamp each envelope.

6. "Teach me how to rumba, Nana!" said Aiden.

7. The nimble monkey climbed the fence.

8. Should Laila be a fairy or angel for Halloween?

Fruity Puzzler

Find the three baskets that contain the same six fruits.

A   B   C   D   E   F

Art by Kevin Zimmer

Art by Ruth J. Flanigan

Monkey See, Monkey Draw

Follow the steps to learn how to draw a monkey, or draw one from your own imagination. Then draw a banana for the monkey to eat!

Yellow Find

The names of **20** things that can be yellow are hidden in this grid—up, down, across, backward, and diagonally. We found BANANA. Can you find the rest?

```
E U V J C O R N N N M T V O Y
C O N S T R U C T I O N H A T
G R U P B Z Y N V C B R E G Z
D R S F D R Q A H A T A E G W
A B Z J R I R I N D I E D R U
F U Y M A W C A O Z B G U L N
F K R R T K N Z I R Y G M E R
O A A E S A Y O L G G Y P M E
D G N T U L E S H I C O T O W
I O A T M C S S Q I J L R N O
L K C U D R E B B U R K U E L
Q P W B Q S E R C T A J C A F
E F V M G D H O V A Z S K N N
L N S U B I C Q U X E M H F U
V I L Q X E H M M I B Y Q D S
```

Word List

BANANA	CHEESE	DUMP TRUCK	RUBBER DUCK
BEE	CHICK	EGG YOLK	SQUASH
BUS	CONSTRUCTION HAT	LEMON	SUN
BUTTER	CORN	LION	SUNFLOWER
CANARY	DAFFODIL	MUSTARD	TAXI

What's Wrong?®

Which things in this picture are silly? It's up to you!

PIN the BANANA

Art by Josh Cleland

What's for Dessert?

This café has tasty desserts that are also code crackers! Each coded space has two numbers. The first number tells you which menu item to look at; the second number tells you which letter in that item to use. For example, the first coded letter is 1-3. The 1 tells you to go to PEACH PIE. Count 3 letters in, and you've got an A. Fill in the rest to find some sweet jokes.

Dessert Menu

1. PEACH PIE
2. KEY LIME PIE
3. BANANA SPLIT
4. LEMON PUDDING
5. MISSISSIPPI MUD PIE

6. SEVEN-LAYER CAKE
7. BLUEBERRY COBBLER
8. DOUBLE-FUDGE BROWNIE
9. WHITE-CHOCOLATE MOUSSE

What's the best thing to eat in a bathtub?

A __ __ __ __ __ __ __ __ __ __
1-3 3-7 1-1 4-4 3-5 4-12 2-2 1-4 3-4 2-1 4-2

Why do doughnuts go to the dentist?

__ __ __ __ __ __ __ __ __ __ __ __
9-4 4-4 8-10 2-2 3-11 8-7 5-2 2-4 4-1 9-3 4-5 8-10 3-7

What's the easiest way to make a banana split?

__ __ __ __ __ __ __ __ __ __ __ __.
9-6 4-7 3-11 5-2 9-4 2-5 6-5 1-5 3-6 7-2 8-7

Check . . . and Double Check

Compare these two pictures. Can you find at least **22** differences?

Crisscross Cone

These **10** ice-cream words will fit into this grid in just one way.
Use the number of letters in each word as a clue to where it fits.
We filled in BANANA SPLIT to get you started.

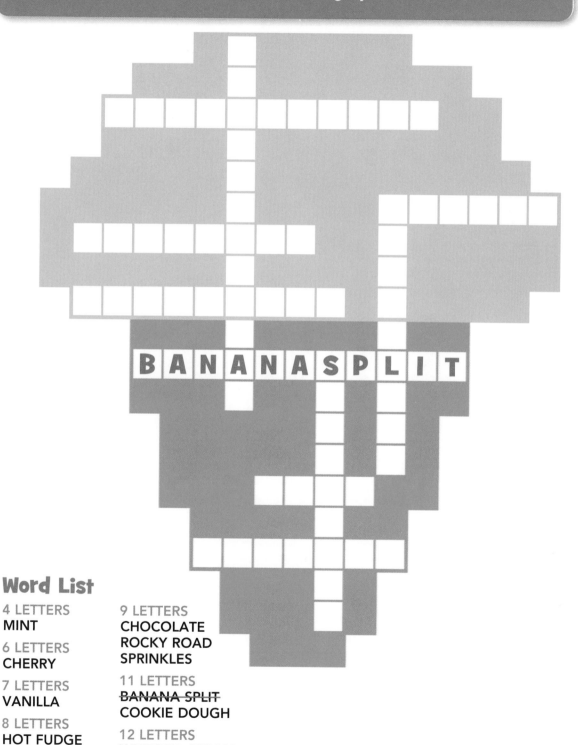

Word List

4 LETTERS
MINT

6 LETTERS
CHERRY

7 LETTERS
VANILLA

8 LETTERS
HOT FUDGE

9 LETTERS
CHOCOLATE
ROCKY ROAD
SPRINKLES

11 LETTERS
~~BANANA SPLIT~~
COOKIE DOUGH

12 LETTERS
WHIPPED CREAM

Fruitville Fun Run

The race is over, but the judges didn't do a *berry* good job keeping an eye on the finish line. They'd be *grapeful* for your help! Use the clues below to figure out the order the racers finished the Fruitville Fun Run.

Can you find the hidden pencil, sock, ruler, and screw?

Art by Amanda Haley

1. One of the red fruits came in 2nd place.

2. Strawberry was in a jam at the beginning of the race, but she made up for it at the end by finishing one place ahead of Orange.

3. Orange ran out of juice and came in last place.

4. Pear finished the race wearing her lucky pair of sneakers, which she bought on a shopping trip with the 1st place racer.

Use the chart to keep track of your answers. Put an X in each box that can't be true and an O in boxes that match.

	1st	2nd	3rd	4th	5th
Apple					
Banana					
Orange					
Pear					
Strawberry					

Tic Tac Row

What do the ice-cream treats in each row
(horizontally, vertically, and diagonally) have in common?

Gotta Split

Can you find four differences
between these two banana splits?

Double Cross

Pirates love *arrrr*-anges, but bananas are full of vitamin *sea*, too. To find the answer to the riddle below, first cross out all the pairs of matching letters. Then write the remaining letters in order in the spaces at the bottom of the page.

TT	BB	CC	AA	WH	PP
SS	EN	LL	XX	TH	KK
EY	YY	DD	OO	BB	RE
MM	ON	FF	EE	LL	QQ
BB	JJ	SA	SS	GG	RR
JJ	CC	HH	PP	IL	UU

Can you find 5 hidden objects in this scene? They all can be found in a classroom.

When do pirates buy bananas?

__ __ __ __ __ __ __ __ __ __ __ __ ,__

__ __ __ __ __ __ __ __

Banana Split or Splat?

The kids on the swim team bought ice-cream cones after the big meet.
They want to treat their coach, too! If they pool their change shown here,
do they have enough to buy her a banana split?

By Diane Boykas • Art by Kent Culotta

Two of a Kind

Can you find the two banana splits that are the same?

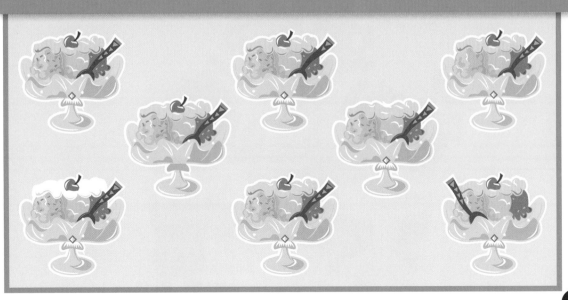

Art by Clay Cantrell

A Tasty Treat

Each clue below leads to an answer that can be made up of letters from the words FROZEN BANANA. Can you pick the answers from the bunch?

FROZEN BANANA

1. An animal with black-and-white stripes   __ __ __ __ __

2. Where farm animals live   __ __ __ __

3. An extremely bright color   __ __ __ __ __

4. The number for nothing   __ __ __ __

5. A covering or wrap to wear   __ __ __ __ __

6. To work to get something   __ __ __ __ __

7. A medal for third place   __ __ __ __ __ __

8. The opposite of far   __ __ __ __ __

9. A sports or concert space   __ __ __ __ __

10. Your birthday is on the day you were __ __ __ __ .

This Maze Has A-peel

Take a bite out of this banana by making your way from START to FINISH.

START

FINISH

Art by Tom Woolley

Going Bananas

To solve this puzzle, look at the pair of numbers under each blank. Find the first number along the orange row, and the second number along the blue column. Then find the banana where those two numbers meet. Write the letters you find in the blanks. We did the first one to get you started.

10	A	N	W	O	V	B	P	S	S	J	T
9	X	Q	D	N	E	C	L	N	A	C	P
8	U	K	P	X	D	D	I	I	B	A	L
7	L	E	D	C	G	Q	S	H	O	P	Z
6	Q	W	C	D	A	R	V	A	H	Y	Q
5	T	A	N	U	F	A	A	K	M	R	B
4	V	O	N	R	R	N	G	X	O	S	C
3	C	B	V	K	H	P	G	R	P	W	E
2	Y	E	N	O	S	L	T	E	Q	E	F
1	R	U	T	H	Z	E	I	E	X	Y	L
	1	2	3	4	5	6	7	8	9	10	11

Why don't bananas get lonely?

T __ __ __ __   __ __ __ __ __ __ __   __ __ __ __
3,1 9,6 8,1 1,2   6,5 7,9 2,6 6,5 1,2 5,2   9,6 6,5 3,5 7,3

__ __ __ __ __ __   __ __   __ __ __ __ __ __ __ __ .
6,5 4,4 9,4 1,8 3,5 3,9   8,8 3,5   11,5 1,8 3,5 4,7 9,6 8,1 5,2

Art by Xiao Xin

120

Hello, Yellow!

These **14** yellow items will fit into this grid in just one way.
Use the number of letters in each word as a clue to where it fits.
Ready to go for the gold? Yellow gold, that is!

Word List

3 LETTERS	5 LETTERS	8 LETTERS
BEE	CHICK	DAFFODIL
SUN	LEMON	**9 LETTERS**
4 LETTERS	**6 LETTERS**	GOLDFINCH
CORN	BANANA	SCHOOL BUS
TAXI	BUTTER	**10 LETTERS**
	CANARY	GRAPEFRUIT
	OMELET	

Fruit Code

There are three jokes about fruit on this page.
Use the picture code to fill in the letters and finish the jokes.

A   B   E   F   I   L   N
O   P   R   S   T   U   Y

What do you call two banana peels on the floor?

What do you call an apple that plays the trumpet?

What do you call a cat that eats lemons?

Art by Mike Moran

122

Costume Party

Zoe and her friends each brought a different snack to the costume party. Using the clues below, can you figure out which snack each friend brought and what costume he or she wore?

	Banana	Pink Fairy	Blue Fairy	Superhero	Caveman	Cake	Chips	Popcorn	Veggie Tray	Fruit Salad
Zoe										
Kayla										
Adam										
Stella										
Hunter										

Use the chart to keep track of your answers.
Put an X in each box that can't be true and an O in boxes that match.

1. The girls who came as fairies brought snacks that start with the same letter.

2. Zoe dressed up as her favorite fruit and brought a snack that includes that fruit.

3. Adam thanked the caveman for bringing his favorite snack, popcorn.

4. Kayla decorated her cake with pink frosting to match her costume.

Chocolate Banana Pops

Here is a tasty recipe to try!

1. Peel 4 **bananas** and cut them in half (across). Place them on a cookie sheet lined with wax paper.

2. Put a **wooden craft stick** into the cut end of each banana. Place the tray of bananas in the freezer for about an hour.

3. While the bananas are freezing, ask an adult to help melt 1 cup of **semi-sweet chocolate chips** in a double boiler or in the microwave.

4. Remove the bananas from the freezer. Carefully dip them into the melted chocolate. Cover them with toppings, such as **granola, candy, nuts,** or **sprinkles**.

5. Put the bananas back on the cookie sheet and freeze for 3 to 5 hours. Eat and enjoy!

Art by Mike Dammer

Laugh Out Loud

What do you call a monkey
with all his bananas taken away?
Furious George

Why don't bananas snore?
*Because they don't want to wake
the rest of the bunch*

What did the banana do when
it heard the ice cream?
It split.

What fruit contains barium
and double sodium?
BaNaNa

Knock, knock.
Who's there?
Banana.
Banana who?
Knock, knock.
Who's there?
Banana.
Banana who?

Knock, knock.
Who's there?
Orange.
Orange who?
Orange you glad I
didn't say *banana*?

Maddie: On a traffic light, green
means go, yellow means wait,
and red means stop, right?
Elle: Yes.
Maddie: Well, on a banana, green
means wait, yellow means go,
and red means, "Where did
you get that banana?!"

Art by (from top to bottom) Rich Powell, Kelly Kennedy, and Pete Whitehead

B-B-Bananas!

Bananas buying balloons and Bring blue bananas both have three words that start with the letter **B**. What silly phrase can you think of that can be described with three **B** words? Draw a picture of it here.

Riddle Sudoku

Fill in the squares so that the six letters appear once in each row, column, and 2 x 3 box. Then read the yellow squares to find out the answer to the riddle.

Riddle: What key opens a banana?

Letters: **E K M N O Y**

					O
E			Y		M
K			O	Y	
	E	O			N
O		M			K
			M		

Answer: __ __ __ __ __ __

A Bunch of Paths

These diners are enjoying the yummy fruit salad they ordered, but they have plenty to share with a friend. Can you find the right path to the table? The symbols will tell you which way to move. Don't slip on the banana peel!

Move 1 space **DOWN**

Move 1 space **LEFT**

Move 1 space **RIGHT**

STOP

Path 1   Path 2   Path 3   Path 4   Path 5   Path 6

Art by Mitch Mortimer

Hidden Pieces

Can you find the seven jigsaw pieces in this photo of bananas?

The Case of the Missing Bananas

These monkeys are working on solving an important case.
Can you help them find **16** multicolored bananas hidden in this picture?

Art by Mike Dammer

Answers

Page 2

Page 3

Page 4

Page 5

Page 6

Page 7

Page 8

Page 9

Page 10

Answers

Page 11

Page 12

Page 13

Page 14

Page 15

Page 16

Page 17

Page 18

Page 19

Answers

Page 20

Page 21

Page 22

Page 23

Page 24

Page 25

Page 26

Page 27

Page 28

Answers

Page 29

Page 30

Page 31

Page 32

Page 33

Page 34

Page 35

Page 36

Page 37

Answers

Page 38

Page 39

Page 40

Page 41

Page 42

Page 43

Page 44

Page 45

Page 46

Answers

Page 47

Page 48

Page 49

Page 50

Page 51

Page 52

Page 53

Page 54

Page 55

Answers

Page 56

Page 57

Page 58

Page 59

Page 60

Page 61

Page 62

Page 63

Page 64

Answers

Page 65

Page 66

Page 67

Page 68

Page 69

Page 70

Page 71

Page 72

Page 73

Page 74

Page 75

Page 76

Page 77

Page 78

Page 79

Page 80

Page 81

Page 82

Answers

Page 83

Page 84

Page 85

Page 86

Page 87

Page 88

Page 89

Page 90

Page 91

Answers

Page 92

Page 93

Page 94

Page 95

Page 96

Page 97

- We found 5 apples (including 2 apple cores), 8 wedges of orange, and 3 bunches of grapes. There are more wedges of orange than apples or grapes.

- The spoons are on pages 2, 5, 7, 21, 22, 25, 41, 45, 47, 49, 50, 55, 56, 57, 62, 63, 72, 74, 75, 76, 80, 82, 83, 84, 85, 88, 95.

- We found 8 slices of bread and 9 muffins. There are more muffins.

Page 100

Page 101

```
P L U M Y V X E B Z C C E R C
K E K I B A N A N A T X L K G
B Y R R E B W A R T S L J R I
A N A T M T J S P S M H L Z F
H P Y L I M E D E W U C M P E
M F P U M R U P A N N C U X A
Z J U L N O A M C A G E M Y R
N Z F O E R R S H N O L E M R
F B M L G C Z A P U M E A C D
N E X J B X I T N B J R H E Y
L N T O C I R P A G E E R S R
G R A P E F R U I T E R R Y R
U U I O P A P A Y A E R Y O Y
I E N M D N M B C X H Y J Y K
G W M K I W I S R T S K W K E
```

Page 102

"Max could order Banana Bread, a Banana Fruit Salad, and a Banana Cream Pie. He could also order a Banana Fritter, a Grilled Banana Sandwich, and a Banana Custard Cupcake. What other combinations did you find?"

Mei: Frozen Bananas
Miko: Banana Split
Monte: Banana Cream Pie
Mille: Banana Custard Cupcake

Answers

Page 103

Page 104

The youngest monkey is 7 years old, the middle monkey is 21 years old, and the oldest monkey is 42 years old.

Page 105

Why did the orange go to the doctor?
IT WASN'T PEELING WELL.

What are bananas best at in gymnastics?
SPLITS

What are twins' favorite fruit?
PEARS

Page 107

1. "One more lap, please," said the coach. (apple)

2. A trip to Waikiki will be fun. (kiwi)

3. Kate and Penelope are best friends. (pear)

4. Eli meant to water the plants, but he forgot. (lime)

5. Please stamp each envelope. (peach)

6. "Teach me how to rumba, Nana!" said Aiden. (banana)

7. The nimble monkey climbed the fence. (lemon)

8. Should Laila be a fairy or angel for Halloween?

Page 109

Page 111

What's the best thing to eat in a bathtub?
A SPONGE CAKE

Why do doughnuts go to the dentist?
TO GET FILLINGS

What's the easiest way to make a banana split?
CUT IT IN HALF.

Page 112

Page 113

Answers

Page 114

Apple: 2nd **Pear:** 3rd
Banana: 1st **Strawberry:** 4th
Orange: 5th

Page 115

blue bowl, banana, spoon
cherry
whipped cream
sprinkles
cookies
chocolate syrup

Page 116

When do pirates buy bananas?
WHEN THEY'RE ON SAIL

Page 117

Banana Split or Splat?
Yes, they have $3.77 (which is 2 cents more than they need).

Two of a Kind

Page 118

1. ZEBRA
2. BARN
3. NEON
4. ZERO
5. ROBE
6. EARN
7. BRONZE
8. NEAR
9. ARENA
10. BORN

Page 119

Page 120

Why don't bananas get lonely?
THEY ALWAYS HANG AROUND IN BUNCHES.

Page 121

GOLD
TAX
DAFFODIL
CORN
GRAPEFRUIT
BANANA
BEE
CHICK
SCHOOLBUS
BUTTER
CANARY
LEMON
OMELET

Page 122

What do you call two banana peels on the floor?
ONE PAIR OF SLIPPERS

What do you call an apple that plays the trumpet?
TOOTY FRUITY

What do you call a cat that eats lemons?
A SOUR PUSS

Answers

Page 123

Zoe: banana, fruit salad

Kayla: pink fairy, cake

Adam: superhero,
veggie tray

Stella: blue fairy, chips

Hunter: caveman,
popcorn

Page 127

Answer: M O N K E Y

Page 128

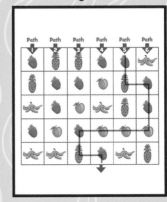

Page 129

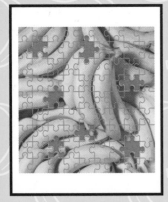

Page 130

For information about permission to reproduce
selections from this book, please contact
permissions@highlights.com.

Published by Highlights for Children
P.O. Box 18201
Columbus, Ohio 43218-0201
Printed in China
ISBN: 978-1-62979-942-1

First edition
Visit our website at Highlights.com.
10 9 8 7 6 5 4 3 2 1